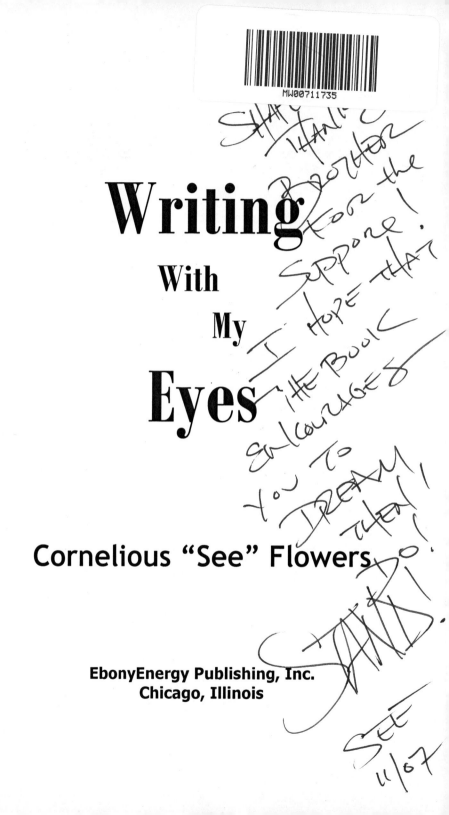

Writing
With
My
Eyes

Cornelious "See" Flowers

EbonyEnergy Publishing, Inc.
Chicago, Illinois

Writing With My Eyes
Copyright©2007
Cornelious Flowers

EbonyEnergy Publishing, Inc.
Permissions Department
P.O. Box 43476
Chicago, IL 60643-0476

Although the author and publisher have made every effort to
ensure the accuracy and completeness of information contained
in this book, we assume no responsibility for errors,
inaccuracies, omissions or any inconsistency therein.

Any slights of people, places, belief systems or organizations are
unintentional. Any resemblance to any person living, dead or
somewhere in between is truly coincidental unless otherwise
stated.

ISBN: 0-9755092-9-2   ISBN 13 Digit: 978-0-9755092-9-6
Library of Congress Control Number: 2007920833

Cover Design & Layout: Mark Ingram of MAITECH Interactive
Graphics and layout contributions by
Barron Steward of Steward Designs
Editor: Lynda Bruce

Printed in the United States
First Printing
EbonyEnergy Publishing Inc. (NFP)
www.EbonyEnergyBooks.com

Dedication

This book is dedicated to the memory of

Michelle Tamara Flowers

and

Mildred James

Mother, thank you.
Grandmother, thank you.

This book is possible
Because of my Father,
Which art in Heaven
And His Son,
Who art in us.

This book is for Coron Tremayn Flowers
Baby, Daddy loves you and will do everything he can
for you, give everything he has to you and follow
every word with an action to inspire you.
Thank you for saving me.
Yours are the eyes I write with.
DAD

can you SEE?

DREAM, then DO!

Acknowledgements

Family

I must first acknowledge every ounce and fiber of my being, existing because you loved me. Thank you Father, Amen.

Mother, the best is yet to come. I know you are here. I see you in your children. Thank you.

Tweet, you inspire me to be a great man so that I am at least an example or an inspiration to someone else. I love you. She does know. Jeremy, I love you. I hope you know that. April, you are one of the strongest women I know. She is proud of you. Janice, happiness is an outfit, but you can wear it when you want to; everyday if you feel like it. Hope, thank you. Turk, honk the horn for me! Felicia, you are blessed.

To my grandfather whom I may never meet, thank you. I heard you were a poet, are a poet. Now, I know where it came from—down the street the whole time. To the many family members I have that I know and don't know. Call me. Good to know who you are. Rock, you didn't have to, but you wanted to and for that I always had a home. I love you. Mayn, my father, I will be because you wouldn't and I don't know how to explain how much I love you for that.

Friends

Renee Vaughn, there are no words, I prayed for you. Mrs. Diane Dwyer, you made me write my first real poem. Who knew? (By the way, this is in no specific order). Joyce Little, thank you. Thank you so much. Andrea Anderson, I'm sorry; she made me do it. Eric Kellogg, Mr. Mitchell, My Uncle Bubba (Morris James)—real men. Her, for him. Vinnie, stop using that word! Get ready! Blade's Barbershop: Self, some say, some do. Slim, thanks for firing me (That's what it felt like at the time). Scoot, change is instant. Sharon, strong black woman. Thornton Township High School. Hillcrest High School. Rosa L. Parks Middle School. King Elementary. Southern Illinois at Carbondale. Alcorn State University, these places taught me language. Harvey, Illinois; Markham, Illinois; Robbins, Illinois; Atlanta, Georgia; Chicago, Illinois; Lorman, Mississippi; Louisiana (not sure which part), these places taught me life. Eric, Queen, Family, Ron Scott, Real Man (Stop them at the door), Byron, Kevin A. Williams (WAK)—the hottest artists on the planet. Byron, stay busy. Kevin, you are history. You are the future, I'm glad I know you. Chicago artist(s) poets, rappers, singers, visual artists, musicians, I believe in us. Orron Kenyatta, Triple Blak, J. Ivy, DeWolfe, Deanna Dean, Lamont (Well Verse), Enigma—Real Brothaz unite (I left some of you out—Got another book on the way). Tip, meet me somewhere. Sponge Bob, thank you. Robert and Debra Martin, I love you guys so much and will never not be here for you. Thank you for my first taste of that tax bracket. Thank you for adopting me so late in life. Yinka, you sparked this revolution.

A very special THANK YOU to Mark Ingram and his staff; Mark, thank you for being an example of God's unquestionable love for us. Thank you for everything from then to now to when. Delisia, understand I know who you are and you mean the world to me. Thank you for encouraging me. To Thelma, what if I didn't have a car and you had a suitcase?

God Is Good

That sister in IHOP, Lord knows. Tiaralyn, strong. LeRoy McMath, for that opportunity. Dionna Griffin, for that chance. Davida, there is a poem in here for you (I had to say more). I know so many people. So, I'll just list some, Thank you: Meishelle, Carmen, Shady (Terry), Roland, George, Dreena & family, Devona, Jewel (you are), Kellogg's, Craig's, Flowers', James', Latham's, Robinson's, Lewis', Presswood's, Jones', DePillar's; Families, I better not forget the Whatley's! Black Ice (Philly), Talaam Acey (NY), and speaking of New York, New York is beautiful. People get out of your area and go see the world. I bet Africa is amazing. Little Aaron, I hope you dance—Love, Mr. See. Every church I've visited, every congregation I've joined. *The power of life and death is in the tongue, growth to every ministry that does just that. Success to every individual who seeks God first and then realizes you must first do for self—Beliefs, Actions, Words. You must know you are in control of your destiny. So understanding to you, Peace to you, Happiness to you. "I see it, so I say it. I say it, so I see it." Progress.

And so that I don't forget, ORIGINAL PRODUCTIONS, Thom Beers, DISCOVERY (TLC specifically), all of the people that got a chance to experience "THE MESSENGERS" series, thank you for watching that leg of my journey. And to all of the *Messengers*! (This book had already been done, I will thank you all personally in the next one).

Others

If you feel as though you've been left out, email me:

findme@seethepoet.com

www.seethepoet.com

www.myspace.com/seethepoet

*Thank you EbonyEnergy! Cheryl, Steve, Lynda, Chris, Sarah, Kennedy. Much Success!"

Table of Contents

can you SEE?

DREAM, then DO!

Introduction

A poet once told me, "To whom much is given, much is required." I was about nineteen at the time and to the surprise of many, this was the first time I had ever heard what I now know to be one of the most affirmative, inspirational and so frequently used quotes in the history of language. I found it to mean several things.

One, that anything you are given requires extreme compliance and obligation of duty—Someone gives you a job, you have to work. Two, at the time it seemed to mean from one person of stature and fame to a potential adversary or mentored that the price of the buddy system is paid when rewards surface after inclusion. I felt as though he was telling me that if he takes me under his wing, I must answer his knock at my door when and if he came. This was the "I scratch you, you scratch me" speech inserted into privileged little kids sometime before adolescence or at least I got that much out of it. Third, obedience, I felt that this meant if GOD gave me my destiny, I must give Him my desire. I must be obedient and find my purpose in line with His plan.

Really, while this man was talking to me, I formed these ideas. It is as if those words spoke to an ear I had never used before. I heard my calling and my purpose and my fears. It has taken me seven years to script these thoughts but I now have true meaning and definition to what the words, "To whom much is given, much is required" mean to me. When he, who has found his purpose has found himself 'eye deep' in it and has developed passion for it, he must put himself in a position to receive full value of what destiny has appraised his life at. He must be ready to, rather, he must assume only responsibility. He must be accountable. He must give as he has received, listen as he has talked, run as he has walked. He must make a choice and then do. So, I have written my first book. I once was told that GOD had given me the gift of understanding, furnished inside the home of poetry or spoken word and language inside the costume of writing. So, I must explain—I must spend my existence writing down the thoughts of my soul and find purpose in spreading the good news of what my GOD has done for me and his promise to all.

Now out of that initial conversation, I received this—as poets we are given the ability to translate into words, the thoughts, actions, dreams, hopes, aspirations, failures, intentions, messages, passions, goals, feelings, and fears of our societies, of our cultures. We are given the responsibility of balancing the wager of life and death on the scales of expression throughout art. And with this gift comes the suffering of dedication and sacrifice. The specific negligence of free will for the sincere application of obedience. We must decide to be a vessel guided by will and not want, obligation and not obsession. Purpose and not performance. The reward is honor in nobility and finding just in its cause. Many of us may never find the acclaim we seek nor deserve, but must continue forward for it is the mind that translates the art that defines the true success of any artist rather than the body of works one completes. I have been given before me a great task—*To See.*

To interpret, To write for my life—*with my eyes.*

can you SEE?

DREAM, then DO!

can you SEE?

DREAM, then DO!

Writing With My Eyes

Eye have since *eye*'ve saw
Seen scenes so wrong
That *eye*'ve seemed so in despair
When destiny seems so long

Seen murdered mother's son
Seek solace in seclusion
Seen baby's father seldom bother
Come to see him using

But not without his senses
Since his *Seyeght* have so much to say
Eye have seen his sister crying
Eye have seen this just today

Silhouettes of saddened sombers
Serenade with sour views
Sick of wanting to see him win so badly
Might as well just see him lose

Save his sorry for his *seyelence*
Eye've seen him celebrate his *seyeghs*
They will celebrate his failures
Won't they celebrate his *treye's*

Or see him *wreyete* about his worries
Give him hurry towards his call
In his song, his psalm, his story
Is where he *wreyetes* about them all

And *eye* am just his shadow
Several steps in my disguise
So he cannot see me writing
For *eye* am
Writing with my eyes

LOVE Poems

*"I have written these just for you—
for every woman who desires the
satisfaction and reassurance that
comes with Love, for every man who
can offer this to her..."*

—Cornelious M. Flowers, III

Love Is Just That

Love is just that amazing
You see, love is not only lying down with my woman
Love is waking up and finding you there
Love is just that beautiful
Not only is love seeing you cry
Love is my knowing the reason why
And love is your knowing the extent of my pride
Love is just that interesting
You see love is two kids being curious
And as adults knowing when not to be so serious
Love is not always recognizing the obvious
But realizing that there might be a problem
Love is just that demanding
Love is instantly knowing our song
Love is accepting the fact that if either of us falter
It now becomes our wrong
Love is just that confusing
It's sort of like your doing something I find funny
But me not laughing until you say it's amusing
Love is just that strong
When we don't agree, you side with me
And now I feel so guilty because I was so wrong
Love is just that forgiving
Remember the day we met
It seems you won't let me forget
Well love is the moment I saw you
And my palms began to sweat
Love is just that quick
Love is everyone knowing that I am in love
Even though I deny what must in my face be shown
Love is you taking this little boy's heart
And making him feel so damn grown
Love is just that mature

It's like the first time I met your parents
The mood was so rigid and tense
It was the way you held my hand
I needed no more evidence
Love is just that plain
Even when I played those silly games
You never said game's over
Love is every time I need a pillow to cry into
You replace it with your shoulder
Love is just that unbelievable
Why not tell the world
That which my soul cannot contain
Love is when we are lying down
I begin to strain
You always know just when to call my name
Love is just that erotic
You don't question my whereabouts
And since you love me we never had to shout
Love is just that peaceful
Now that I know what it is about
Even with hope of one day having children
You let me invest in silly ideas
That could never amount to millions
But in the end allowed me to claim
This foundation we were building
Love is just that responsible
I might have never known love
But you gave me the room to explore
And for just that let the record show
I love you even more
So if you find yourself searching
For a reason to stay home with me tonight
Love is just that

Do You Remember Yesterday?

Do you know what was so
Significant about yesterday?
What was so outstanding that
It left me dazed until now—wondering
If I'm supposed to be here,
Watching my words so that I don't say
Too much when all I want to say
Might not be enough,
Do you even have a clue?
Well, yesterday was the last time I saw you
Yes, I know we are to meet again tonight
But yesterday was the last time
So let me ask you
Do you remember yesterday?

To the naked soul it might not seem to mean much
But yesterday I was blessed to have your company—
In a time of need, caressed by the warmth of your
Presence—even in moments when we didn't touch
If I could find a word that said I could love you,
Would you ever believe such?
Do you remember yesterday?

When I woke up this morning,
I placed a pillow into my face
In hopes that it was the one you
Had lain upon the other night
And had somehow left a trace
Just this scent put me back to rest
And when I finally awakened
The pillow was laying on my chest
When will you take its place?
Do you remember yesterday?

Once on my knees
I asked the Lord to send me
A woman who respects all I wanted to do
Who would love me for being me
Someone to help me find the answer to questions
Which left me no clues
I turned to the Lord because
I no longer wanted to choose
And I realized yesterday that he sent me you
And there is so much more I want to say
But right now, I just want to know . . .

Do you remember yesterday?

Do You Know What You've Got?

I watched you in the shower today
And as the water trickled down your spine
I thought quietly to myself
Yes, this is all mine
But do you know what you've got?

On the surface you've got what it takes
To yearn attention
And yes, people stare
I've even mentioned you in my sleep
And someone heard me
Because when I woke up, you were right there
But do you know what you've got?

And not just a body that deserves applause
Even being born with that face
That carries no flaws
You've got just the right amount of flesh
Suitable for resting in my jaws
Do you really know what you've got?

Physically we were made to be
But if I had been warned of your arrival
I would have shouted make believe
I'd never met a woman who thinks so much like me

I don't want to know where you've been
As long as I know that you're staying right here
And baby if you know what you've got
You know that I'll be here for years
But do you know what you've got?

There is only one word to describe what I'm thinking
Only one way to describe how I'm feeling
If you are characterized not by what you tell
But by what you hide, then what are you concealing
Damn, do you know what you've got?

Someone should tell you what you've got
Before this situation gets out of hand
And I'm not going to wait, being the person that I am
Do you know what you've got?
You've got a man

I Don't Understand

See what I don't understand is you've allowed this
man to saturate your ears with what you call game.

And though you were hinted at his deceit you
continually subject yourself to his reign—being
overwhelmed by his pain.
And I don't understand.

He didn't call last night nor did he visit the night
before. And when asked of his intentions and to
explain himself he replied, "What for?"
Yet, you still opened the door.
And I don't understand.

You've never met his family; you've never heard of
his friends and your most frequently asked questions
just happen to be, "Baby where've you been?"
But he's leaving again and again.
I just don't understand.

You don't go out. He just spends the night.
You fuss, he shouts. Yet, everything's alright.
Sweetheart, you've been throwing stones at me from
the window of a glass house with no fairy tale ending
in sight
And I'm trying to open your mind with all my might
But you don't understand.

You sing a song of a better day
Yet, you've begun to believe
That there is no other way
I wonder if he hits you
And if he doesn't, when he does

Will you stay?
It's a harsh reality, but what more can I say
when I don't understand why you love him or why
you defend his every move
I don't understand your reason for staying in a
situation where your only option is to lose
I'm not saying give me a chance
but there are so many others out there to choose
Baby, he's got you looking like a plumb fool
And I don't understand.

And I don't want to understand because it has not
been good for you
My only advice I guess is that you somehow find
yourself and unto yourself you remain true
Because if you don't think you need help, then
there is nothing I can do
Because I don't understand.

The First Day Forever

To have and to hold until death do us apart . . .
I do.

For better or for worse, every moment
from the start . . .
I do.

And as long as you have in your heart to see us
together, then for my part, *sweetheart*,
I promise to give you the first day forever.

I promise to make every day better than the day
before. More words to say I love you
Because . . .
I do.

Even more than yesterday
When I knew nothing like this
Just how good it feels to be right here, right now—
I vow to make every moment like this.

Many women say many men change after awhile;
and while this may be true,
I stand here to say . . .
I'll do.

I'll do what it took to get you every day,
until the day after forever with no regrets.
I promise to always be the day after the day
before we met—no exceptions nor misconceptions.

I'll be who you thought I was,
what I know I am, where I'm supposed to be
until that hour when you say leave—
no *mis*-directions, no split objectives
or ulterior motives.
For all I know, all I know is what I know to be true
and all that is that I know I love you
So when you and your girlfriends get together,
you can tell them how your man has always been
that first day forever.

Still listening to you and still sending flowers
Still calling and staying on the phone for hours
Still opening doors and pulling out chairs
Still acting like it and not just saying I care
Still asking you out and going that extra mile
Still finding a joy in just making you smile
Still making romance a romantic thing
Still making sure you never have a need
Still holding on to your hands and never letting go
Still enjoying kissing you and not afraid to let it show
Still asking for a dance as if he never asked you
before
And the two of us still dance until we're the last
ones on the floor
Still saying I love you because I can't stop it
Still making love to you every chance I get

Can't stop it—can't stop this feeling
Can't stop this dire need because you're all I need
And these are my vows to never be back then
but to always be right now
Even on bad days because it will only get better
and love will only leave if we let it
And I will never let it go

If I ever get mad, I will never let it show
Because you deserve better
and better I than he that doesn't know
Why plant a rose that doesn't grow
These words are seeds that I will forever sow
And this marriage, my reap, will forever grow
because I'll never give you anything less than the
first day forever.

And Just Like That

After years of confusion and misunderstanding
Through hard times so endured, my patience was
demanding
We are still standing
And just like that—you leave

What did I say that you didn't believe
What did I do so wrong, or at least
would have you conceive
that I was untrue—or could it have been you?
And just like that—we're through

I've been honest beyond the truth
To see the love that my heart carries for you
You needed no burden of proof
But what's the use, and just like that
You could throw away all we've been through

I could understand if I had received a sign
Or if we had grown apart from each other
Because that happens sometime
But just like that—you are no longer mine
How could that be?
I would forfeit the gift of eyesight
So that you would see
But I can no longer plea
Your mind is already made up
And I've already been through the same stuff
So, I'll get over it—
Just Like That

You and I

As long as you and I
Have hope for you and I

Then none shall come between
the force of you and I

If there is doubt in whomever
other than you and I

I say they have a fight against them
to destroy us—Let them try

As long as you and I believe in you and I
Believe me—nothing will ever come between
the force of you and I

You Leave Me No Choice

I've tried to notice you noticing me
But that was to no avail
You probably feel the way I do
But you would never tell
So you leave me no choice

I've tried to leave hints and clues
But all I got was smart remarks
If you do really see what I'm saying
Then how could you make me stop
So you leave me no choice

I've tried to impress you, not with materials
But with my mind
Men may fall before your feet a dime a dozen
But a good man is hard to find
So you leave me no choice

I've tried to hold back my advances
So I may seem sensitive or even afraid
But I don't want you to get the wrong idea
I want you to know that—
I know I'll want you everyday
So you leave me no choice

I've tried to be kind
I've tried to be all you say you need
I'll never change my mind about you
Because I know we were meant to be
So you leave me no choice

I've tried to say this in person
I've tried to get you to understand
But when will I get your attention
So that I can be your man
So you leave me no choice
But to take this time and
Do what I should have done long ago
You've left me no other choice
But to love you
I just had to let you know

I Don't Need A Reason

In a few days the candied hearts
Will have all been devoured
The sweet smell of assorted roses
Will no longer captivate the senses
And instead will seem stale and sour
The batteries inside of talking cards
And teddy bears will die in strain
For loss of power
But I will still love just being with you
Every chosen moment
Every given hour
Because I don't need a reason

How could you ever accept this gift of lingerie
Along with a box of chocolates
And this flattering bouquet?
My gift is supposed to mean everything to you
And this is all I have to say
I'm trying to illustrate my undying love for you
Is this the only way?
I love you unto infinity
And this is not the only day
So I don't need a reason

Until next year
Some won't again receive such emotion
And after all of the hysteria
Some will curse this as just commotion
After Victoria has sold every bottle of
"her most fragrant lotion"
I will still have this devotion
My love for you does not need boasting
I don't need a reason

How can one day be held accountable
For a year's worth of desire?
Unlike the 24 hours celebrated
In the name of couples
My love won't expire
I burn like the bush with eternal fire
And to tell you
I don't need a fancy telegram
A newspaper ad, nor a wire
I don't need a reason

Happy Valentine's Year Sweetheart
Oh dear sweet love of mine
I'm not trying to downplay the significance
But I can't just express in this one day
How much I love you all the time
Every follicle on my head
Down every vertebrae of my spine
Beneath my feet on which I'd walk the finest line
I didn't need an explanation
I didn't need a sign
I don't need a reason
You can have your material wish
For if I could, unto you I'd sacrifice the greatest gift
But let's not just celebrate on this day
For in fact I've composed a list—
Every day of every season
For I love you, and I don't need a reason

Her

GOD
The reason I believe in her
HER
The reason I believe in GOD
In her eyes
I see the desire to deny the results of years of
research
She as a woman in these times had evidence as to
the reason why
As relationships we hurt
So why all the men she be diggin' be dirt?

Why a waste of time could only describe the amount
of time every man she had ever given time to be
worth?

But this was my time
Time to defy what was once known as odd
By giving her life through the eyes of a man
Who saw her only as a wife without those lies
That men would normally lie down beneath her
Showing her that I didn't want to keep it real
But instead my intent was to keep her
By giving my all and even more
In hopes that she could realize that we both had
been hurt before
And now between us lies an even score
And to make this work would take hard work
But would not be hard
As I intended to make her my goddess
By giving her my God
God, the reason I believe in her
Her, the reason I believe in God

Yes, sex was in the picture
But only after I had become a permanent fixture
In her emotional mixture
I had hoped to stick with her rather than just stick
her
With a seed of mine
Too many times I've seen babies become babies'
daddies excessively in a shortened length of time
I had hoped to prove to her that longevity and
commitment were both strengths of mine along with
faith, honesty and trust
We would pass that test of time

Time after time testing her endurance
While she was testing mine
While in the back of my mind would occur the
Thought that I could outlast her for just this time
It seems that I always got to the point faster
Because I am blessed in mind
But keep in mind we haven't even had sex
Not just one time
Our conversations are as wet as the falls of Niagara
When I called it was not of want
But because I had to
Sometimes I just had to
Make sure that this was not a dream
And in fact I had you
Thank God

God
The reason I believe in Her

Her
The reason I believe in God...

She had my back like a chair
Like reality, she was just there
Whenever I needed her, I didn't need to ask
She would just care . . . to . . .
Dare . . . to . . . share with whomever
Her persistence and patience
Was what put us together and once put together
We would stay put forever
Putting behind what held us back and
Putting before what made us better
Need—why let her provide
I'd better do better than the best
That had ever been done
In her is the only reason the West had ever been won
She is *The right one baby* . . .
If there had ever been one
She would be the morning star
If there had never been sun

But sometimes I dwell in the past
And I reminiscence about the time
We asked each other
To become one another's last
And promised to compliment each other as such
Sweetheart—
I am the window of life
You are my glass
You keep out what is unwanted in
While protecting our foundation
Like a coat of skin
Metaphorically speaking
Through thick and thin
You let in . . . side of your soul
A man who already knows
The difference between right and wrong

So we may disagree, but we won't fight long
Before you submit to defeat
I'll admit I'm wrong
In the head
I'll admit I'm gone
But you inspire the fire that burns
Inside the pits of my loins
I don't know how I got here
But with you, I know where I'm going
I planted this seed a long time ago
I'm finally reaping what I've sown says God

God
The reason I believe in Her

Her
The reason I believe in God

That's What They All Say

So what is it that *they all say?*
That this time will be the last
But did anyone ever tell you that
If you ever became in need of anything—
You won't have to ask

I plan to be here until a day after forever
I miss you less when we're apart
And more when we're together
Because I just don't want to see you go
There's reassurance in my pride
Since you've joined my side
And I just wanted to let you know

So did *they say that?*
The word commitment puts a fear in my soul
That leaves me trembling
Every time I think of being alone
I'm disillusioned by the actions
Of those before me that laid burden upon your soul
I think you would have to be blind
To treat this woman I see so wrong
But I guess *they all say* that

Was it by fate that these paths of ours should cross?
Leaving my state of being
Torn between pleasure and pain
And ending up lost
I must have been lost
Or how could I explain finding you
If love is having you on my mind all the time
Then maybe I'm in love with you
But I guess they all say that

And they all tell you how beautiful you smell—
My queen draped in fruits of passion
The nectar of your body wash
Leaves my senses in a trance
And your body—
Is giving my lips more things to talk about
As in the moonlight our shadows dance
I should be writing about—
The things going on in my pants
If I were a tortoise right now
I'd be popping out of my shell
Has any man ever told you that?
Could he have ever said it so well?

But what don't they all say
And I shall use those words to explain this pain in my
chest when you're gone
Or this knot in my stomach
That has my temperature rising
Just because I called your house
And you didn't answer the phone
Yes, I know it's hard but you have to first believe
That we can work
And if we try together it won't be long
Privacy fences and ceiling fans
Those are just some of the small details
I've included along with you in my five year plan
Next to God, I want to be the reason you open your
eyes in the morning, not just your man
Tell me that you understand
But don't tell me what *they all say*
Because it really doesn't matter to me
If you didn't like what was said the first time
By the first man—
Then you should never let him repeat

If it's time you need then I'll wait
Or maybe I'm too close then I'll give you your space
But do you know what the funny thing is
That's What *They All Say*

Let's Do Jamaica Again

I see you basking in the Jamaican sunset
Even though you stand beside that body of water
I wonder if your body has ever truly been wet

I often forget that you belong to me
But this Jamaican sun as it reflects against your skin
Has made me see
To trade places with every grain of sand
That sits beneath your feet I'd give anything

Yes . . .
I do believe

The Jamaican air carries your scent
And I stand hypnotized
I am captivated—
By every strand of hair that blows along this wind
As you walk along the beach towards me
I want so badly to freeze this moment
I try to withhold my Jamaican nature rise

This is beautiful
I would travel a thousand seas
To once again have this chance
In this Jamaican paradise as I and my woman dance
Oh, Sweet Lady—
Let's do Jamaica again

I Just Want to Say I Love You

Sometimes I just want to say I Love You
And sometimes I just like to be on the phone
And even though we're doing little bits of nothing
Sometimes I just like being at home

And sometimes I say the wrong things
Because I know you'll have your say
But in the end of all we go through
I know you'll have your way

Just want to see you live your dreams
And if I can make them come true
Then all you have to do is give me the chance
And there isn't anything I won't do

We won't make everyone happy
And I'm sure as hell we won't try
Because if we tried real hard to make our love work
Then surely our love will never die

I hope you believe in the spirit of love
Just as I believe in the spirit in you
And I know with hard work and commitment
What is meant to be one will never break into two

So trust yourself to trust in me
Make me your partner and I'll make you my bride
Give me your future as the same for me
Make me a promise to stay by my side
And just know that sometimes
I just want to say—
I Love You

Do Believe I Do Believe I Do

And that's all you have to do
Not be concerned with all that's going on
All that has taken place
Nor all that we are going through
You just—Do believe
I do believe—I do

Never let doubt become the shadow that shades us
Because *what if* will never matter
When we accept GOD as the reason that made us
He can situate; He can save us
And if we retaliate, he shall blame us
And I know this as true
You just—Do believe
I do believe—I do

One should never have to settle
As long as one is satisfied
And one shall appreciate every experience
When it can't be said one has never tried
We can look forward to a life of happiness
For that has never died
And I am proof
You just—Do believe
I do believe—I do

Through memory I have achieved the will of fate
And some things might be misunderstood
But there are no mistakes
A mustard seed of faith—that's all it takes
If you give it your all then all is at stake
And what can you do?
You just—Do believe
I do believe—I do

You Are So Silly

Has a man ever called you the morning after
And every morning after ever since
Ever since that night before that morning
You made him moan
You made him long for more mornings like this
For on this morning and every morning ever since
He's called to say
"Baby, I don't know what to say."

You see, this morning is more morning
Than any morning ever
It doesn't matter whatever happened before
Because this morning we're together
And whether or not it's important to you
I just got this feeling
I've got something important to do
And you would understand if you were me
And had a girl like you
And one morning you woke up and realized that
You knew what everybody else wanted to know
And you had been
Where everyone else had wanted to go

And you were going back and had plans to stay
And every time you wanted to explain
How wonderful you felt
You forgot what you had to say
Because every time you thought about her
You thought about yesterday
And you . . .

Has anyone ever made love to you
Like you've made love to me?
Darling tell me, for it is he I would like to meet
So I can say to him *Na, Na, Na, Na, Na, Na*

That's What I'm Talking About

Do you still remember teaching me how to love
for the first time?
After we made love that first time
You held my hands for sometime after
Looking into my eyes hoping to capture
The moment I was paying the most attention
And that is when you mentioned
The first time you knew

And you made it clear
That it was more than my desire
To have you that had you near
I had only been used to back pocket love
But you gave me Stevie Wonder's *Rocket Love*
Simon says, Momma make you stop it love

Do you still think about how many times
This love made you miss appointments—
Gave you disappointments?
All the nights you got down on your knees
And told God how this is pointless
But you still loved me—
And never took it away
All the misunderstandings—
We moved past
And it only took us a day

Do you ever wonder if I was the right choice— if I've
ever made you doubt the love I possess for you?
Then listen and you will see what I say—
And hear I'm sorry for my voice
Because I still remember how much you mean to me

Every time I breathe—
Every time I leave your presence
I'm reminded of your essence
And every lesson I've learned throughout
Real love
That's what I'm talking about

I Will

To have and to hold you
From now until my dying day
I will

To appreciate and provide
To hold true to my promise that I will stay
I will

To give you every ounce of my being
To offer you nothing less than all I possess
I will

To be sincere in my effort to please you
Promising nothing but my best
I will

To hold you when you need it most
To care for you as I would my own
I will

To believe in your aspirations and dreams
In their pursuit to stand firm
I will

To love you...
To cherish you...
To make certain that we shall forever be
I will

To make sure that this vision
For us is shared mutually
Between you and me
I will

And We'll Dance

Yes . . .
And hold your hand tighter with each beat
And pull you closer
Until the threads of our jeans meet
Let's dance
Move with the melody of the rain drops outside the
window
Let's dance
On top of one another
Behind each other
And then slow
At the bedside in the shower and
On the kitchen floor
Look into my eyes
Whisper into my ears
And ask for more
Dance with me my love
To our favorite song in the dark of night
On the wings of an angel
In the midst of flight
Yes, I'll take this dance
But only if you promise
To play this song again
I'll play this song for you, my woman
You play this song for me, your man
And we'll dance

If I Could Let You Borrow My Heart

No more tears will explain how I feel
I can't describe the frustration
Building heavily in my chest
Or the questions that burden my soul
When I lay my body to rest
But if I could let you borrow my heart
I would no longer have to explain myself

If I could let you borrow my heart
Then you'd know the urgency
That calls for undivided attention
And you wouldn't wonder why
I Just stayed home last night
Or the reasons why I've fail to mention
Certain events or why I expect you to listen to what
I said and know exactly what I meant
If I could let you borrow my heart
Then all you've ever wanted to know
About me will become evident

Were there sparks the moment we met?
Does your touch really make me sweat?
All of those special days shared between us—
Did I ever really forget?
If I could let you borrow my heart
Never again would you become upset

Because I didn't know
The right time to be apologetic
Or for not seeming to be serious
And instead always poetic

If I could let you borrow my heart
You'd know what it felt like to
Envision being a romantic
I only want the best for the two of us
And I know sometimes I seem distracted
Or always in the mood to fuss
And it's not you that I'm afraid of
But I've been hurt before
And I don't know who to trust
But I'm willing to make a brand new start
Somehow, I just wish
I could let you borrow my heart

INSPIRATIONAL Poems

"He that is inspired is he that accepts the responsibility of hope."

—Cornelious M. Flowers, III

Our Past

Civilization is like a game of chess
As complex as the human alphabet
And once put on paper
The alphabet becomes civilization's medicine

But did you know . . .
Civilizations, chess, the alphabet and medicine
Along with paper that document our regimen
Were all invented by Africans
And you can stand on your own two feet
Thanks to W.A. Deitz
He invented the shoe

As a matter of fact
The rotary engine, automatic gear shift
And motor
Air conditioning unit
And starter generator
Helicopter
And elevator
Clothes dryer and lawn mower
We invented them too

Cleanliness is a godly notion
And thanks to George Washington Carver
We've got soaps and lotions
And when Isaac R. Johnson
Invented the bicycle frame
He put millions in motion

The wonderful folding chair
The brush that dresses your hair
The hair dressing device and pressing comb
The refrigerator and programmable remote control
Refrigeration and pace maker controls
Even the bathroom commode
The folding bed and postal box
Dust pan and household mop
The typewriter and the ordinary lock
The door knob and the door stop
We don't stop...

The fire escape ladder
Electric cut-off switch and telephone transmitter
The galvanic battery and auto air brake
Roller coaster and electro mechanic brake
The electric railway and telephone system
Along with the relay instrument were all good
And all were invented by Granville T. Woods

The planter for cotton and corn are results of
Henry Blair being born
And a sister named Sarah Boone gave us
The ironing board

The super soaker and the eye protector
Electric lamp and the clothes dresser
The fire extinguisher and old fashioned lantern
Even the pot that cooks with pressure
Are all African American inventions

And music would not have come as far
If Joseph Dickinson had not invented
The Player Piano
Or the arm for the record player
Or Robert Fleming Jr. had not invented the guitar

The heating furnace by Alice H. Parker
The gas burner by B.F. Jackson
And the defroster by Frederick M. Jones
All help to keep us warm
And where would we be without the gas mask
And traffic signal by Garret Morgan
The airship or what you call a blimp
The fountain pen, the hand stamp, even the kitchen
Table and the household wrench

And so that weapons would hit harder
Otis Boykin invented the guided missile
And H. Bradberry invented the torpedo discharger

I wonder if Tiger Woods knows that the golf tee
Was invented by someone who looked just like me
We even invented ice cream
And so many other things

But we're led to believe that in order
To be successful we had to dream
Well this is not a dream—we invented these things

We are so much more successful than just the black
quarterback or short stop or starting point guard
Even more than just those beautiful voices that sing
We are kings and queens—

Descendants of a superior being
Who is responsible for our being
So one day we will stop just being
And see reality
Because in reality
There is only one certainty—our past
And without knowledge of our past it will be gone
So pass it on

Rain

When lovers meet again in Heaven
And begin to rekindle moments
That made it all worth it
It rains

And when we find ourselves
Not finding time for ourselves
To enjoy one another
It rains

When our loved ones leave us
And look down upon us while crying
It rains

And when we believe in the
Belief that God will never leave
And as long as we need
God will be
It rains

And sometimes it just rains
Because we love the way it feels
Falling down upon our faces
When It rains

Held
(A Monologue)

Son:
And she stood there in front of me in agony
Asking me ...

Mother:
"How could he hurt me?
I gave him Heaven
He gave me heartache and herpes
Where was his decency and how could he desert me?

He said he would light my fire
And he actually burnt me . . . but I stayed there.
After endless evenings, regardless of my well being,
My neck housing his heavy breathing . . . I laid there.
What was supposed to be a beautiful place we were
traveling to ends up him coming—though
I have never made my way there . . .
He stayed out . . . I just stayed fair
And now this is what I've turned my back on God for.
This is what, regardless of my back,
I've worked so hard for—something he couldn't even
get hard for.

And I'd rather be held—I'd rather be held in the
arms of a man who cares about my well-being rather
than being well off.
And often I try to get him to see that I believe in him
because I believe in God and God is screaming child
just get him to me.
So I look way past his past
And I only asks questions I know the answers to

Because I know his leaving will stop my breathing
quicker than cancers do—not realizing that he is a
cancer too—rapidly breaking down because that's
what cancers do.
But I believe in God and I'd rather be living wrong
than left alone and even though he's in the
bathroom with the door closed—on the phone—
At least he's home.
And rather than follow my first mind
I'd rather let him lead me on.

And I pray that what he says is true
because I believed his every thought
and that's why I tell my sister that we had fought.
Rather than saying he had beat me again
because jealousy was a woman to him
And he had seen her again
And I had found out
And he blamed me for doubts
That I had every right to.

So then he said that love was complicated
And his parents had fights too
And well that's the way his dad had beat his mom
And I had tried to be his mom
So this was all my fault, not his mom's
And it's so confusing
But so is losing—*this man.*

And I'd rather be held by this man who holds me
It may hurt sometimes
But he holds me
Every time he finishes arguing
He holds me

And when no one else is around he holds me hostage
I gave him a beautiful baby boy
And he gave me bondage
And then he kicks me out
And he says you won't take my child away
And the last time he kicked me out
I hadn't seen my child for days
And I know my son would rather be held
And I never wanted my son to see his father in jail
And I know the pastor at church so well
And I wouldn't want him to think that
I had failed at marriage
And that would be so embarrassing to my family
Who I hadn't seen in awhile
And it was less because they were living in Denver
And more because I live in denial
Where I have been living for awhile
Once I told my sister that he was just like our father
And now my sister agrees
Saying he treats you like his child
What about you?
Well, I just wanna be—held
And he promised that he would hold me
So when he pushes me
I say I fell
And when he makes me sick
I say I'm well
And when he threatens to kill me
I never tell
Because he loves me
And he never means by any means
To do anything other than love me
And that's why we took those vows
And we're getting so close now
Even if it's either he's going out

Or I'm going down
I really don't mind
And he constantly tells me
That he's the only one for me
And somebody else
I really won't find
And I know he doesn't want anyone else
He just really wants time
Maybe I smothered him
I thought I was just understanding
But maybe I mothered him
My expectations here just way too high
Maybe I covered him
But I can't believe he left me
All this time he's loved everyone except me
And I give you my word
As God as my witness this will be the last time
He walks in this house and you can quote me
Dammit, the coroner will be carrying him out!"

Son:
Wait a minute . . .
Mom, that's my father you're talking about
And what could he have done so wrong
How could you have stayed so long
Because now I'm just like him
Maybe you should have walked away
But you stayed just like him
And now my walk and my ways
Are just like him
You never let me see inside so inside
I only saw what you let me see
And now I see
You would rather just let me be . . .
Leave him

Believe me, if I had known or it was up to me
I would have said, "Leave him."
But now you expect me to believe that
He's not who I thought he was
And not because he has another identity
But rather evidence from inside of the man that
I tend to become . . . yearly
I can't see you going on hurting . . . hardy
But mom you're asking me to part
With a part of me
And that I can hardly see
Why'd you wait?
Why didn't you escape before
I knew who he was?
I just heard you say
You knew who he was
And Then She Said . . .

Mother:
"Son, It's because I rather be held . . ."

The End of War

Bloodshed in the midst of confusion
While anticipation awaits illusion
And wild souls capture lost souls
Both steadily losing faith
People no longer wish to fate
But enlist to hate
The pace of broken heartbeats
Is melodic to chase . . . but wait
How is thy hope reduced to helplessness?
Maybe selfishness
The seed might fall as far as the wind blows
But if never planted, it never grows
Bloodshed no more
Confusion no more
Illusion, what for?
I anticipate the end of war
For love is the reason for
Lack or maybe abundance of—either or
But love will be the reason for
The end of war

Friends

Friends don't need excuses or reasons
Friends don't need special occasions
Nor certain seasons
Friends just need you to believe in

Friends don't need special recognition
Friends don't need request or permission
Friends just need love without condition

Friends don't need to be taught
Friends don't need to be bought
Friends just need affirmation
That for them you've fought

Friends don't need doctors
To know what ails us
Friends don't need evidence
To know who fails us
Friends just need that feeling that tells us

That they are friends

True

A Great Man

His soul desire is to provide for family
Amidst controversy speculation
Or the compassion that comes in understanding
Sacrificed will be his honor, his pride
And his status all for the well being
Of those who walk in his shadows

Yes, a great man
Like great men before him
He will have dreams, but as a great man
Will know the consequence of fantasy
And will by any means celebrate
The joy of being blessed just to have
Opportunity and this will reflect
In his mentality

True great man
For his children he will
Become the hero fairy tales depict
Allowing himself to exhibit his manhood
Physically, emotionally and spiritually
Asking of them not to achieve what fulfills his spirit
But only to work at their best ability
And to his wife will become her protector,
her brother, her father and her guide
And with these qualities
Confidence will reflect in her stride
Work of a great man

For his family
This man will show no barrier of love
Incapable of harvesting the hate that encounters
Our heritage and pride
Instead this man cares
And for answers it is in the Lord that he confides
This is a true great man
Amongst this great man in me sits others
Who as great men themselves
Will exemplify the style that is respected
Questioned and feared by others
Great men I would like to call brothers
Because for us a great man will have no limits
For his nation he will lead troops into war
And if requested will stand in the background
And allow everyone else to enter the door
A great man

Great yesterday, great today and great tomorrow
A great man will ask questions as a leader
And will be heard when he has to follow
A role model not just for children
But for young and old together
This man won't be great for the time being
This man will be great forever
He's a great man

I Will Survive

No longer will I shed tears in sadness
Greatness requires strength that is
Far greater than this madness
So I will not fight the fight of those
Who lost the fight for not fighting back

But I will not stand back
I will not stop searching for my truth
For what was meant for me is far greater
Than the wrath of my enemies
And their presence is proof

And I will not ignore the interpretation
Of the part through my elders
For what they have seen is my future
There is no need to look elsewhere
I will not neglect the needs of those in need
And so the Bible I read
Though I will not read between the lines
And find reason to no longer read

I will not lose faith
By chasing the reality that lost faith because
It has faith that faith would be lost
I will no longer hold inside
Contempt for those I despise
Nor will I try to rise above hostility
So that I will not forget humility

But I will not forget
I will not forget, I will not forget
And I will not give in to temptation
I will not forget patience
And I will no longer rush to judgment
For what is truly no obligation of mine
And I will no longer criticize character
For that is truly a situation of time
And I will no longer take time, but give time
I will no longer take care, but give care
And I will no longer be deprived
But I will survive

Meant To Be

I was emancipated by racists

Shackled by bigots

Murdered by my kind

Mocked by my peers

Ridiculed by society

Ignored by legislation

Abused by Law Enforcement

Sheltered by my parents

But now I understand

I was meant to be

Will You Be Ready

Even when it gets here
You won't be ready
For the revolution

And when it comes
You won't face it
Because you will run
From the revolution

Just like the sun on a rainy day
Or succulent T-Bone on an empty plate
You won't be there
When—Oh, here it comes
Duck!
The revolution

Don't be scared
Not of the revolution
Nor fear the prosecution
Of the idea
The thought of restitution
That comes near with the revolution

In your dreams even
When you feign
And desire the thoughts
Beware even our ancestors talked about the
revolution

When our baby sisters
Those who lost their virginity as prostitutes
And the little brothers
Who succumb to the gang

And learn the language
Both using slang in anguish
There is only one hope
The revolution

Don't just see the revolution
Don't just be the revolution
You must breathe the revolution
No need for resolution
Just prepare for the revolution

There won't be problems
Only solutions
As the wicked spin
That inflicts its kin with sin
Will witness

She may come in the form of a woman
Or it may be another form
Maybe a book with pages torn
But you won't research it
You'll read about it
And then
Together
We'll shout
Revolution

Can I Get Some Change

Do you have any spare change?
Rather can you spare some change?
So spare is change

I just need a little change to buy
Me some—time

You thought I might buy me some wine
But I don't even drink

You are so quick to say you thought
When you almost never think

I'm on the brink of drowning in poverty
And everyone's frowning but nobody's stopping me
Nor is anyone stopping these
Sisters of mine from crying
When no one notices them trying
Until notice is posted of them dying

It's hopeless if your focus is on finding
Reason to believe in something other than binding—
Together

The dollar might get you far—but change is forever

Can I get some change?

Too many men become daddies and not fathers
Because too many women
Would rather "we not bother"
But if we are too far apart already
Then we can never get farther—
Ever!

Sisters we can listen but we can't talk together
But if we listen
We can walk together
My argument is
You can't argue forever

I need a little change

And then I could get some change
By changing the way things are steadily changing
But since things are steadily changing
I just hope to do my best
Unfortunately, I don't have any change left
And I'm tired of saying pain and change in the same
breath

Too many of us have low self-esteem
If you know what I mean
Maybe because they don't know what I've seen
Or where I've been
Does anybody realize that everybody sins
And there has to be a loser if somebody has to win?

Change is a game
Everyone has to get in

But we're not that far from it
The problems is Jesus, Buddha, Aesop, Aristotle,
Sahara, the Dali Lama, the Pope, Ghandi, Zen,
Confucius, and Muhammad
So busy trying to find something wrong
That we never find a summit

Maybe if we could meet together
Then we could see together
Change is something we'll see forever

So can I get some change?

Money doesn't mean a thing
If all it does is buy things
Make the money mean something
Try things—like making some change
While you're busy claiming that steak
I'm staking my claim
So in exchange for giving me money
They won't be taking my name
Keep the dollars—I'll take some change
All them dollars are nonsense
When my people are in pain
How can you move while your people stay the same?

Can I get some change?

FAITH Poems

Faith—"But what is courage without fear, the same as dreaming without faith."

—Cornelious M. Flowers, III

My Prayer For Success

Dear Lord:

Guide my steps as I travel this road
Where all I desire walks with all I know
As I pursue my destiny
And follow my dreams
Would you inspire my wants and allow my needs
Could you show me favor that outweighs my faith
So that if I falter, you keep my pace
In my journey that will take me far and beyond
I pray for your constant protection
That will keep me unharmed
I pray for wisdom, I pray for growth
I pray for patience which I need the most
Rather you're my foundation before family and
friends
For I can be assured you'll be there at the end
And in return, my Father, I give you my best
And I ask that you answer
My prayer for success . . .

Amen

My Days Will Get Better

As I hold heavenly my head
My tears are dried in the burning sun
And I am reminded of the Lord's grace
As for me he has sent his only one

So my days will get better

Nor my sickness, neither my prosperity
Can overshadow my God's mercy
For it is thorough in its clarity
Because His word was sent in sincerity

So my days will get better

Doubt stands only in those blinded
And the cold shoulders of greed, envy, and jealousy
I never mind it
More than likely—in His name
If you seek, you shall find it
And I hold these thoughts forever

So my days will get better

Anchored

In the Lord
My soul rests there safely
By the sword
So there is no if, no but, no maybe

In His word
My attention resides right there
By the herd
He is my shepherd, standing right there

In His grace
Which is sufficient, satisfying and steady
By His goodness
Which is always great and for that I am always ready

In His mercy
Which I was granted way before I was deservant
By the salvation
Which I was rewarded for being His servant

In His kingdom
So unto all of His riches belong to me
By the promise
That His gratuity is my guarantee
He in I and I in He . . .
Anchored

I Can't Complain

I no longer try to stake my claim
For I am truly blessed in Jesus' name
So I can't complain

When things don't turn out quite the way I meant
I don't give in, for I am a gift—heaven sent
So I can't complain

I no longer look for ways to detail God's glory
The Book is my tool, His word is my story
So I can't complain

When I pray it is for thanks, I expect no return
For the gift is early in the morning
When with His spirit I burn
So I can't complain

I might not walk a straight path
Nor look both ways for danger
But along this darkened road
I know my God is no stranger
So I can't complain

So I won't complain, for He owes me nothing
But somehow, someway
I ended up with something

And I can't complain!

Storm

There was no wind,
But there were worries

There was no rain
But there was resistance

There were no clouds
But there was confusion

There was no precipitation
But there was persistence

There was no thunder
But there was tragedy

There was no lightening
But there was darkness actually

There were no signs
But there was significant destruction

There was no warning
There was no shelter to get under
And I endured just the same
Though mine was not of physical pain

Some asked, "How did you do it?"
Well, it was still just a storm
My Lord brought me through it

ENCOURAGEMENT Poems

DREAM, then DO!
I encourage you to become an
example of hope. Don't say
impossible, say I'm POSSIBLE.
Speak life at all times and live happy
in this moment."

—Cornelious M. Flowers, III

Somebody Knows

If you believe in love, happiness will find your heart
And if happiness is what you seek
Love is just a start

If you search for understanding
Then seek the elder's song
For one who's learned from your mistakes
Shall never guide you wrong

If trust in another may offer satisfaction
Then trust in yourself
To be judged just by our actions

If you yearn an authority of spiritual power
Then trust in God for His fruit shall never sour

If you look for friendships with opposite of evil
Then carry within yourself
That you seek of other people

If of these things you are all composed
Then know in your heart that somebody knows

Keep The Faith

It might be hard to believe
And most times extremely hard to see
And sometimes you'll find yourself discouraged
And in doubt for certain is just so hard to be

You will stumble and fall many times
But never give in to adversity
I can tell you first hand
Sometimes I feel so alone
It's as if someone is cursing me

Trials and tribulation
Come before triumph and the taste of success
But in due time comes your season
And you shall rejoice
For you have endured the test
For grace is sufficient
And mercy is the reason you've been blessed

Weeping may endure for a night
But joy cometh in the coming day
Just hold on to our Lord, Jesus Christ
And indeed, keep the faith

In The Ghetto

In the ghetto
The trigga's quicker to let go
Quicker than hearin' the hood
Say Hello
In the ghetto

Stilettos become step ladders
To step-daddies
Some are down to be anything
Except daddies
In the ghetto

Little girls lose their virginity
Before they lose their baby teeth
Seeing sisters sacrifice their souls
Is something I hate to see
But I look
In the ghetto

We work for welfare
But who the Hell cares
In the ghetto

Could be leaders become followers
Should be verse spitters become swallowers
Not believing politicians but buying into politics
In the ghetto

Crack means cash flow
So stash yo' dreams
Just like Satchmo, you better just breathe
In the ghetto

'Cuz ain't nothing like it
You can ride rims, Tims or bike it
Some of just white Nike it
In the ghetto
That's just how I like it
In the ghetto

They got country clubs and garden spots
We got liquor stores and barber shops
In the ghetto

Big business is still settled by hand shakes
And you can get killed by the wrong
Signal your hand makes
In the ghetto

You can be jealous and just playing at the same time
Bring a N***** up and put a N***** down
With the same line
In the ghetto

And where I'm from looks just like Baghdad
Looks just like Palestine
We're at war
In the ghetto

Peace time went out with the peace signs
We used to wear around our necks
Gain knowledge, lose respect
In the ghetto

Life is inspired by the motion picture
Get the soundtrack
To the ghetto

Speaking of music
Why can't we use it for the movement
In the ghetto
But where else can I get what's mine
Then lose it . . .
But in the ghetto

Dream

Maybe he just wants to be a fireman
And not the first overall draft pick
And she doesn't want to be a Williams sister
Because she would much rather
Be a podiatrist
And they both like fun and games
But all they want to do is play
And enjoy what comes with being children
Even the mistakes—
And even making them
But instead we're making them make choices
At such an early age that
Will indeed hamper their destiny
And ultimately decide their fates
And that's our mistake
Because they just want to dream
But instead we'll put them on those teams that
Teach them that individuality is just some scheme
That streams far from the schematics of teamwork
Well, unless they excel in gymnastics
And then that would be an extension of teamwork
And with that comes hard work especially
If you want to be the star or the best which would
Take an individual effort nonetheless
And it probably doesn't make much sense
But just imagine how much cents it really makes
And since as adults we've basically lost our chances
We tell them that we know what it really takes
So we really make them not regret
The choices they'll make
By not letting them make any

Because we know what's best for them
And as far as risks go they won't have to worry
If they don't take any
And when it all boils down to it, just growing up is
hard enough without—it'll take plenty
So let them dream

Let them dream, while they can
Because they can and because they're supposed to
And let them become who they want to
Because they want to
And not because we want them to
But because we should want them to be their best
Regardless of whether or not is suits our interest and
They're not interested in the "finer" things
They just want to dream

Our fascination with impulse
And instant gratification has left our children
'Grade less' and without graduation
The sensationalism that captivates our minds
And bodies has embodied an entire generation
And so they're left with music videos
To motivate their minds and costume jewelry
To decorate their lives and that's all a dream
But not like the dreams we used to have
They don't have a chance to dream like that
They can't imagine being a doctor
Because the family doesn't have one of those
And well they could have wanted to be a lawyer
Because their family has had some of those
And I suppose they might want to be a pregnant
High school drop out because mom was one of those
And dads are either someone to fear
Or someone to talk about and those

Are not reasons you're giving
Those are excuses
You are using to walk out
And where are our grandparents
Why is my family tree so transparent?
Why are the people who made it walking away?
Where are the examples of progress
That lead us to stay put?
Why can't we put those things away
That have no place in plain view?
How dare you get mad at a 17-year-old dad when he
blames you?
It's sad when I and segregationists share the same
view
I don't think we understand
That when something ails us
There are those who care about us
Feeling that same pain too
So, let them dream

Let them dream while they can—because they can
And because they're supposed to and let them
Become who they want to because they want to
And not because we want them to
Because we should want them to be their best
Regardless of whether or not it suits our interest and
They're not interested in the "finer" things
They just want to dream

He doesn't want to be a street pharmacist
And please don't be alarmed
But he'd rather be a journalist
And write about how drugs
Have dried up his community
Where those thugs hang usually

That's where the grade school used to be and now
The only things the kids learn there
Is how to earn money
But money can't buy back morals and self-respect
That we've lost over the years
And for some reason we've made him feel guilty
For aspiring to be different and called him a sell-out
For standing out above his peers
And when he finds a young woman, we don't tell him
All she is—we tell him all she isn't
And no matter what he sees in her, we remind him
of where she's from
And tell him that she's no different and as for her
She doesn't want to like living life
The way she has been
Because she's seen how those girls turn out
Thirteen-year-old, turned-out has-beens and since
She was three she has been told
How beautiful she was and how she should be on TV
And all of this time she's had to equate what made
Her feel good with what's on TV
And yes she's so cute and tall, but she doesn't want
to be a model
Because she wants to follow in the footsteps of
Harriet Tubman and there's something even to be
Said about that—for some reason all we know of our
history is what they told us
And so most of us as children never knew that our
ancestors were soldiers—only that we were slaves
And they never tell us
What some who came before us did—they only teach
us what they couldn't do
And after a lifetime of hearing things like that
Anyone could probably end up lost, wouldn't you?
They've taken away our dreams

And now back to her because she sees past that
And it is our responsibility
To help her move past that
But it seems that whenever there is a beacon
of light along the way we have flashbacks
Of those dark times and we result to
Techniques used against us then prejudice was used
Against us when someone realized how to take away
Our dreams, but that should have been too hard—
even when they tried to use GOD—it should have
been useless then
And now, it's no different when plantations have
Become prisons and they could no longer use
Segregation so they started to use systems
And now they use TV and SUV's
And they let us buy the chains to place around
Our necks and get them made from precious metals
And camouflage them as respect and our little ones
Desire to be branded so they make them worth
A check and never tell them what they really cost
So they'll never know what they've really lost
And they see us do it, so they
Believe in what they've been shown
But we don't teach them that certain things
Are not important until they've been grown
But maybe that's our fault for falling in line
Thinking that we're finally standing in the world
When we've been falling the whole time
I feel so bad for these kids
Because we want them to take part in the parts
We missed and we've put a numerical value
On the heart in a sense
You can't manufacture dreams—I'm convinced

Maybe he just wants to be a fireman
And not the first overall draft pick
And she doesn't want to be a Williams sister
Because she would much rather be a podiatrist

So let them dream

She Deserves Better

(For Davida)

She deserves better
Than any man that would let her
Not be herself
It was her self-determination
That set aside my faults
And brought love
Brought hugs and kisses
To someone who thought love was distant
I thought love was isn't
Isn't the right time; Isn't the right one
Isn't— wasn't—really not
But isn't she the one who gave me what I've got
And doesn't even have it herself
She doesn't have love
Because she gave mine to someone else
And she deserves better
She still wants happily ever after even after all this
When what was supposed to be all bliss
Went bust
Something about what went wrong with us
And now I understand
What she fears about marriage
A wonderful son and another man
But on the other hand
She needed that
To have and to hold
She heeded that
And the past is just what it is
We can leave it that
She deserves better
And yet

She still believes
Still believes in herself
And it was her self-preservation
That kept her waitin' rather than giving in
Other than living in
Self-pity
She still believes
So she's still giving him
Self-esteem
Even though it seems that all he gives her
Is selfishness
But her selflessness gives her steam
To press on
And she doesn't need 'Maybeline' or 'press-ons'
She got God and kept goin'
Everybody needs a bottom to keep from fallin'
And even it gets stepped on
But she deserves better
The perfect mother to a son that will be taught
To look beyond the surface
To look behind the person
To find purpose
And what they stand for, for she's still askin'
If you can't be a husband
What you wanna be a man for
If you couldn't take this serious
What did you take my hand for
And for this she deserves better
And better off is where she'll be
When she looks in the mirror and says
I deserve me
I deserve better than
Any man that doesn't have enough
Love for himself
To love me; I deserve better

Freeze, Black Man!

I once heard *The Expression* shouted out
Freeze, Black Man!
Freeze, Black Man!
Before the words had been blurted out
Yes . .Sir
It's absurd that I wasn't mindful of your business
Wasn't it freedom of speech
Or is this
The exemption to the rule
My skin has provided me with
Freedom is the right to choose
My skin has provided me with
Freedom was our fight to lose
And we did
So now I hear
Freeze, Black Man!
Freeze, Black Man!
As tears tour through my pride
That stares down the outside of reality
When all I hear is actually
Fact of the matter is that
Brutality is matter of fact to me—so
Freeze, Black Man!
Before you get sent
To your knees Black Man
Give up your confidence . . .
Please Black Man
Is that all you desire?
The fire behind the dream my brother had
That feeling inside of my dad
That made my mother mad
I thought I was the color
But now I see it was the other—thing

Freeze, Black Man!
But I don't understand
You cherish the idea
That I should perish right here
But because of a thought consistent through all man
I thought it was force behind my black hand
Freeze, Black Man!
You hate not that I can do so much
But that I can
Because I already know I can
No matter the fact that I but mere man
As long as I am, I can still stand
For something
Rather than fall for nothing
When one thing is clear
That I am still here
And the truth is somewhere near
But how can the truth be someone's fear
You fear the truth that I hold so dear
Freeze, Black Man!
Your plan was to dissect my people
Through evil plots and ways
Slavery for a lifetime of days
Prison to rehabilitate my ways
When all we wanted
Was the freedom to stay together
The freedom to say
Whatever
The freedom to be
Forever
However you made impossible that endeavor
By severing the ties
Between us and the skies
But my Savior can come as the devil in disguise
So we rise.

Freeze, Black Man!
Years of your constant oppression
Was just a God-sent blessing
So that we would appreciate the God-sent blessings
You held me captive
But taught me lessons
Through pain we found pleasure
In your trash we found treasure
And what we can now hold so pure
Is that we know we can endure
Forever . . .
Your chains only brought us together
What you provided as terror
Ended up your error
And it only lasted an era
For it will soon be over
And through an open mind
I will soon find closure
On my grasp of Jehovah
Why put your knee in my back
When you can just lean on my shoulder
See, through the blood we are all brothers
This place is big enough for all of us
Freeze, Black Man!
But you can't see that man
That you can be that man
Before color you are just that—Man
Before it was your idea
It was the Creator's plan
You can crush, but you can't create a man
So how can you not love, but hate a man
And now I see your facial smiling
While racial profiling
While me and mine just
Put faith in time

Hoping next time will be the last time
Or maybe before you form an opinion
You would ask mine
And we could make racism a past time
And not a pastime
It's like a bad storm
I just wish would pass by
But in the end
You will have to make amends
But you'd rather make foes that make friends
When that doesn't make sense
But you can't be convinced
Because you'd rather make cents
So, that was your intention back then
And ever since
It's been
Freeze, Black Man!

I Should've Cared More

Dear Son:

I should've cared more
Instead I cared more about myself

When everyone else was saying that you weren't
mine
But I knew all the time

Even though I never minded makin' a baby
There was always something different
About making a baby mine

Add to that the fact that things were never right
Between your mother and I
We were just fooling around
Because that's what fools do

We thought we saw eye to eye
But one eye was intention and the other eye was
Intercourse

And of course I . . . never mind
I should've cared more
Our marriage was based on the fact that I needed
control

I needed to hold on to something because I was
never held on to
Well there were those times when my mamma held
on to me so my daddies—Damn . . . my daddies
She made me call them all that

The way they all used to break in and escape
I wanted to call them cons

Every time the police arrested my momma
They called 'em John
She made me call 'em all daddy

And I needed to hold on to something because
I was never held on to
Well there were times when my momma held on to
me so that my daddies wouldn't get a chance to
beat her face
Like they had always beat her special place
And they would always stop when she put me
between the two

I married your mom because I never wanted this for
you
And I should've cared more

Not long after we got married we realized we were
both people we never really knew
We were different people with nothing in common
but you
By then she was fed up, I was ready to give up and
you were two

We knew everything except what to do
And then we said things
We didn't mean to ever say like
I never liked you anyway

And the whole time you were doing that
I was doing this, and we never realized we never had
much but we had a relationship

So I went about my way
And I thought that being a man was to step away
rather than fight for this semi-family

And I thought that I could deal with just seeing you
Semi-annually and after just three visits
I realized that this just might damage me

And you might think I was thinking selfishly
But I was thinking of a system that had always had a
history of not helping me

And don't think that I didn't call
Because I didn't have anything to say
No son, I just didn't want to go on
Just talking to you once a day

I know I missed your first steps and birthdays
Those were my worst days
First day of school and times you broke the rules
Those were the times I barely made it through
Graduations—your mother wouldn't let me bother
Girlfriends—son I know there were so many
Because I'm your father and therefore
I should've cared more

I should've cared more about my responsibilities,
But my response was always questioned—as were
my abilities—by your mom and her family

She made you a bargaining tool so pardon me
But harmony was something I rather would see
Rather than hearing what I should be and how
Farther along the two of you could be
And how without me you'd be better off

Can you imagine how it feels
To find something but only to find out
that it would be finally better lost
Son, I've suffered at all cost
And every moment since there hasn't been a
moment I haven't clinched my teeth in anger
Thinking you might have been raised by another man
Who had some other plan other than seeing you take
a stance

Other than seeing you take a chance
My plan . . .Was—
Does it even matter?...*I'd rather not*
Rather than tell you all that I know now
I know now that I should have known better than

And even though you might hear all that I say
You may not be listening
and I don't blame you
Son, I should have cared more
Instead I was caring more about—more or less
everything else,
My morals were somewhere else
Everything I had been taught had been tossed
because of the loss of my father and all I got from
believing in God was the realization that life only
gets harder

And the harder I tried to believe in his lies
I found my-self bothered
It was hard for me to get on my knees and pray
because it started... *Our Father*
And often my mother would tell me and my brother
that it would be OK

But occasionally, I'd put my ear to her door and
listen to her pray and she would tell God she was
sorry for lying
And though she was trying she felt it was dying
(that chance that he was coming back) and while
she was crying (I told myself I'd never do that) and
that's why this hurts so much
Because I know better than that
I should've cared more . . .
And I hope this is not in vain

But I've got something I want to say
Son, I still want to play
Catch, tag, and basketball
And I know you're grown
But after all is said and done
I'm your father and you're my son
And without you near, my heart's been sore
But it's my fault, I should've cared more
I should've cared more
Instead I cared more about more or less
Everything else, I had a chance to be a parent and
instead I let your mother have a baby all by herself
and when I should've turned around I turned my
back to you

I thought I knew it all
But didn't know what to do
And although I had a chance in the end
I left being a man up to you
And all of these years you were all
I've ever cared for
But Son now I know
I should have cared more

Just Like Me

I wrote this song for every soldier that just wanted
to stand for something

So he stood for his country on the front line
sacrificing his life while the whole time those bullets
and bombs backfired

He was fighting for a group of guys who gave him
orders to go further behind enemy lines and said so
from the cozy confines of some fancy country club's
back nine

I wrote this song for every sister that never
sacrificed her soul for some—thing
'Cuz if there was one—thing that she was taught
was that she could never be bought
and if she just gave herself away, she would pay the
cost
So, she never got lost in thoughts of buying that
bullsh** that them N****s had brought to her
'Cuz they ain't wanna do nothin' but do her and her
parents had taught her that don't nobody do nothin'
for free
So she tells them 'N*****s' if you can't do better,
you can't do me

I wrote this song for every son that never really got
to appreciate the sunshine—well now except for that
one time a day
'Cuz now where he stays, 'one time', ain't no more
than one minute away

107

He stays in a cage and can only go out to play one
time a day
When he was younger he saw his Mother about one
time a day and he had only seen his dad one time
and one time knew that he had to get by on his own
and all he could do was do that
So he got caught up that one time by one time and
the judge gave him one more time and he blew that

And well, I wrote this song for every man who takes
the hand of some kid
And sees the opportunity for someone to not make
the mistakes that he did
And so he's a mentor and not a meant-to
Like so many men that meant to be fathers
But couldn't be bothered
And never realized that if they could be there
Then they could be farther but they left it to
mothers to be fathers
But this man wants to be bothered with that
'Cuz his father felt that he was a burden and left his
mother with that

So, I wrote this song for every woman that knows she
shouldn't be alone but goes along without
Independent of that dependency that goes without
saying
Never saying that she feels so without
and doubts her beauty inside because it seems that
what's on the outside is all that counts
Yet not even an ounce of her being is being what it
seems these men have meant her to be—she still
believes
Even though she constantly thinks of the man in her
life

And knows that her biggest question is not when
will he take her hand, but when will he leave—
and yet she still believes

And I wrote this song for every teacher, preacher
and police especially the ones that we don't see
those who try so hard but struggle under authority,
wondering—government or God— and every mistake
made by one bad seed now casts a shadow on every
employee

And so we may never enjoy their good deeds and
those that should be punished enjoy a system that
enjoys a plea

And now they have a history of crimes against
humanity and some of them cry insanity
and why is this so damaging
because families die so easily

And so I wrote this song for every fiber that requires
breath—hold on
Life might not go well, but it goes on

And Lord knows, just play your part
from every intention to every start
It only gets better, if you let it
To define your purpose, find your heart
And it might be hard to walk away
but it will be so much harder if you stay
Say what you mean, give yourself a chance
and find room to breathe
And if this doesn't apply to you then I wrote it for
me

I wrote this song for every second, I had to cry
myself to sleep
For every promise, I could not keep
Every vision, I could not see
Every goal, I could not achieve
Every instance, I could not believe
For every conception, I could not conceive
And I wrote this song for everyone
Just Like Me

It's A Sign
(For Amadou Diallo)

In due time my people will no longer be defined
by jail time or chalk lines

Statistically, they can never account for what
happened in our past so realistically they fault mine

But let me ask you—
How can four white police officers in our backyard
shoot at an unarmed brother forty-one times?

It requires no debate, that's just a crime
That's not a mistake my people, that's a sign

A sign that times that have yet to change
And because we're pacified so easily
We are consistently subjected to pain
You see they only acquitted O.J.
So we'd forget about Rodney King
Yes, my country 'tis of thee
Sweet land of liberty
For thee I sing

We as a people have invented a style that out spans
any map
But we don't realize how important we are,
nor the impact
Don't you ever wonder why white customers account
for 63% of those who buy rap?

Don't mistake their interest as confusion
we don't live an illusion

We stay one step ahead of a game
that was designed to keep us losing
And they fear that
We're the only ones mad at the fact that we're
black
We constantly stereotype ourselves
That's the way they want us to act
It bothers me as it should bother you, but please
don't let it
You see that's the problem we have now
We give the devil too much credit
God says we must forgive those who trespass against
Us—Just don't forget it
There's only so much time before all of this is over
We need to use it wisely so we don't regret it

Why is there a fear in me that someone's out to take
what I own?

I've seen my brothers lying dead in the streets
Over materials they can't possess when they are
gone
Don't take for granted the air you breathe
This body from God is a loan
Someone once saw the light that shine inside me—
For this I would like to be known
If we don't try living right, imagine dying wrong
If we don't get it right soon, we won't last long
Many have come before my day and recognized these
very problems
Well, that's the easy part—I'm here to help us solve
them
Because just as those before you
Someone will say they're feeling me
Some will clap their hands

Some will yell in chants
Excuses and lies are killing me
It doesn't take that much mental agility
To take responsibility

We got this far segregated
United where could we really be
Analyze this my people
Only one man was created
How were all men created equal
Oh yes, power is stunning
But Knowledge is lethal

While not only the shortest
But the coldest month of the year
Was given to commemorate our community
We must do more to bring awareness
Instead of being selfish and neglecting opportunity
We must assume only responsibility
That begins with you and me
My only hope is that before it is too late
We see what's right before our eyes
For how can four white police officers in our
backyard shoot at an unarmed brother 41 times

It requires no debate, that's just a crime
That's not a mistake my people
That's a sign

can you SEE?

DREAM, then DO!

LIFE Poems

"L.I.F.E.—I write for those who LIVE—for those who need LIFE—for those who want to enjoy LIVING!"

—Cornelious M. Flowers, III

LIFE Poems

Life is Poetry...Poetry is Life...

Love

Inspiration

Faith

Encouragement

I "See" Life...I Write Life...I AM Life

The following poetic expressions
encompass everything—
Life...

Somebody Say Something

Before he walks out that door
And before he tries a joint
Before he gets drunk for the very first time
Before he makes up his mind to make a point
Before he loses his virginity
Before he gains a reputation
Before he is influenced by the world around him
Before he forgets his way and finds himself waiting
For a bus that'll take him where he has to be
Rather than where he wants to go
Because no one ever paid attention
To him or what he was doing
So before we let him go . . .
Somebody Say Something

Somebody say "Hi" before he tries it
And show him what it means to not be focused
And just remind him that he doesn't need
Marijuana to manifest—rather tell him now
Hemp is hopeless and I hope this is no knock to those
who feel the need to make herbs a dietary
supplement

But I've done a study of my own and statistics show
that an altered state of awareness may enact
subsequent failure and there is no need to tell you
how many brothers have already smoked away
chance after chance to advance in a society that
stands on a platform that pales in comparison to
anything right—but for just these moments we might
want to oblige—if not for our people let's just say
it's for our pride

So we can be proud of him because he stood for
something and couldn't stand smoke

So he never started smoking and as a child he
realized drugs were no joking matter and let's hope
he'll learn an important lesson before he has to find
out the hard way and before we find out what
happens after,
Somebody Say Something

Before he goes out into this world not knowing the
difference between free will and freedom and makes
the mistake of not making the distinction that free
will is from God and freedom is from this country
and once he appreciates the difference he'll know
what it means to hear some things and some things
can only be heard if you listen

So he'll listen to his heart before he listens to his
homeboys and he won't have to look so far for
answers

Friends can give you advice but they can't
necessarily give you chances
This is no dress rehearsal
This is real life—no second chances
He'd better get it real right—right now.

And he might not know that because we didn't show
him and what he doesn't know is what he knows is
way more important than who might know him and
where he is right now is only the starting point for
where he's going and even though he might mean to
mean the best when he becomes a man meaning
means nothing.

He'll have to make a decision to be a man of his
word and that's one thing he's probably never heard
So, Somebody Say Something
Before he walks out that door
And before he tries a joint
Before he gets drunk for the first time
Before he makes up his mind to make a point
Before he loses his virginity
Before he gains a reputation
Before he is influenced by the world around him
Before he forgets his way and finds himself waiting
for a bus that'll take him where he has to be rather
than where he wants to go because no one ever paid
attention to what he was doing
Somebody Say Something

He already has a predisposition to lack thereof—
Lack of funding and moral guidance
Lack of responsible individuals that will hold him
liable and won't just lie to him
Lack of positive reinforcement with examples of
success

Success rather will expose him to poverty and the
notion it suggests—more than likely he'll never hear
from those who made it how to do just that
because those individuals are never so visible once
they move up
They do just that and he's already going to deal with
a father who's invisible
and a mother who holds him responsible for that
and a system that will teach him nothing of his past
and won't prepare him for his future

Don't they understand that it takes more than
nature to make this boy a man
When it comes to his stance, what's in his pants is
useless
But they'll have him believe he can use it whenever
and won't tell him the pain that comes with pleasure
and no one explains that his body is a temple
and that what's down there is a treasure to be found
by someone special—and special ain't the moment
that makes it feel nice—special is the woman that
makes him feel life
By marrying him, she'll make him right
So somebody tell him to wait
Is there anyone that hates to see illiteracy more
than I do?
I'm not saying you have to conjugate verbs and
nouns like I do
But these little young black men sound foreign and
it's almost as if they try to
But that's because we'd rather read them their
rights than read to them at night
We'll wait till they go wrong
Then try to lead them right then blame it on their
songs or their situation
Someone please stand up and be held accountable
an entire generation is waiting and no one seems to
be concerned
So maybe we'll send them to the church
Where the preacher will tell them they'll burn
If you keep trying to hide the truth
Then that's exactly what they'll learn
So somebody Say Something

Tell them that the only thing that matters
Is that he matters in the end

And if he never finds himself
Then he himself will never matter to his friends
And tell him that real men believe in God
And we love one another
And we find beautiful wives because we loved our
mothers and saw to it that our sisters didn't find it
hard to find someone worthwhile and if she has any
glimmer of hope inside herself she'll teach this to
her child and he'll grow up to be the father that I
never had and he'll have respect, honor, dignity and
compassion for the reality is—faith is a concept—yet
one not so hard to grasp
I hope he hears me

Before he walks out that door and before he tries a
joint
Before he gets drunk for the first time
Before he makes up his mind to make a point
Before he loses his virginity
Before he gains a reputation
Before he is influenced by the world around him
Before he forgets his way and finds himself waiting
for a bus that'll take him where he has to be rather
than where he wants to go because no one ever paid
attention to him or what he was doing
Somebody Say Something

Reason

Reasons are predetermined excuses
useless answers to hypothetical suggestions
reckless opinions that originate from fiction or fact
nevertheless rewards for lost thought
Now found
Sounds like . . .
The background of intention
Not to mention
Synonymous to repetition
Or anonymous or politics

Reason being is just reason for the reason why
Or reason if the reason I
Find just reason or just find reason
Reason is the irresponsible gesture of
reasoning with self without help of one's self
instead finding reason to reason with someone else
when there is no reason where there is no reason . . .
unless reason is reason itself

Can you give?
Do you have?
Do you need?
What is a reason behind the circumstance or
consequence?
Reasons are . . . but not hard to get
Reason being
Good reason is hard to fit
Into reason

How can you find season to defy reason
There is no defined reason
In due time we shall find reason

To believe in reason
Or reason to believe in the find of reason
Before time is the reason
Reason is deceased
With so many pieces to get
it is hard to get a piece of reason in peace

Or be at peace
With the reason
That only gave you a piece of a reason
To find peace in reason
Or find a piece of reason that gives one peace

There is no reason
For the reason received in response to the obvious
Of someone using judgment and not reason
To come to a reasonable conclusion
Without even the illusion of having a good reason
To either find or get found out so for no reason
They find reasonable doubt
Without reason to be in what is reason to be out
So I checked my voice of reason
Voice of my opinion was the only reason I needed
To find a reason
To be needed
Or to need any reason you needed to give
To establish the reason you needed to live
The only reason is . . .
You don't need a reason except to find a reason
Instead of trying reason
In lieu of buying reason
Just try eyeing reason rather than denying reason
and realize that life is not defined
By any reason for many reasons
What's your reason?

So What!

So what you got platinum
You ain't got property
And what's happening probably
Is the record company
Is treating you improperly
And for a piece of platinum
You just became property
You call it mainstream
I call it Monopoly
You're stepping out of a V8 or V12
But never stepped out of grade 8 or grade 12
You're supposed to be a made man
But you're just man made
A man who never made well
And I'm not hatin'
For your sake
I'm just taking this time
To tickle (laughter) your mind
For in due time you'll find
That this business is as fickle as Heinz
But best things do come to those who wait
Those who wait for royalty checks
Instead your loyalty is heavily set in hoods and sets
You got revolvers but no respect
And so you've dissolved and the facts reflected in
Your music
You worked so hard to do something
Why work so hard to lose it
You dudes ain't hard, you're fluids
Why should I acknowledge that soft sh** you doing?
I see right through it
Your existence is dependent
On the resistance of independence

through persistence you had a chance to make a
difference
you didn't
Kids infatuated with riches and clothes
Little sisters growing up to be bit**** and ho**
not because they chose to but because you made
slang the status quo
Yeah you had us going
You should have had us grow
You worried about your sound scan
But I don't like your sound man
You got a nation to lift up
But you letting us down man
For what
Get control of your masters
Before master get control of you
Faster than BeBe's kids become bastards
Record labels taking classes is stretching N*****'s
a** holes out like elastic without plastic
this sh** gets drastic
So stop asking for permission
Dreaming for the existence in the long distance of
royalty checks when the fact is
If we left hip-hop today
There would be no hip-hop hooray
Yeah, a lot of money got made
But only negative attention got paid
On our behalf—Do the math
Before you commit
And realize
N******s don't even give God 10%
What I meant was—they giving us 3-5%
of our hard work and achievement
You don't have to believe me, just believe it
How can anyone get any percent of what's yo' s***?

So what you got platinum
You ain't got property
And what's happening probably is the record
company is treating you improperly
And now for a piece of platinum
You just became property
You call it mainstream
I call it Monopoly

You got some chrome 20's
That helped you bone many
A whole lot of fans
And maybe a house in Philly
But you're paying rent
The whole time getting sent
Around the country
Where you spent a lot of money
You left the hood flossin'
But you came back funny
Because the whole time you were submitting rhymes
You were cutting off your publishing ties
Ended up getting your 'AS CAP*ped*' by 'BMI'
Maybe you thought that rap would last
But didn't think your type of rap was a fad
You saturated the streets with that nonsense
And you had it locked
But now you've just been had
Oh you can't tell
You better find a farmer to buy that bullsh*t you sale
This piece was not personal
But if you trying to turn it off
Then I'm talking to you
Stop looking around
And watch what you do
Learn the business

And start talking the truth
If you're out there talking for nothing
Let's talk about what's the use
'Cuz when it's all said and done
Your people remember what you lost
Not what you won
They are concerned with what you're doing
Not what you've done
It's about your fundamentals
Not about your funds
There's enough out here for all of us
You betta' get it before it's gone

So what you got platinum
You ain't got property
And what's happening probably is the record
company is treating you improperly
And now for a piece of platinum
You just became property
You call it mainstream
I call it Monopoly

What She Doesn't Know Is

What she doesn't know is . . .
What she's gonna be
But I do
And I'll do just about anything
To see to it that if she wants to
Then she'll do it
By an means
And I mean anything that it takes
She's gonna make it and I'll prove it
She's been through too much
And I'll lose it if she loses
Because of you or anybody
Else that doesn't do what they
Can to help her move on, so move on
If you're planning to make no
Plans and I swear by no chance
Will no man nor woman
For that matter stand in her way because
She stands for something and
That matters
And for the most part it doesn't matter
These days unless you show the most parts
And the worst part is she's got those too
But she's still at odds with 'stil-let-os'
Because she knows that as tight as she is she can still
let go and what's more important than that is that
they're uncomfortable and they look like that on
videos
and sound like that on radios but she knows that we
like that and yet we know that that's not true
We'd rather see her in her 3rd semester at U of I
and not her 3rd trimester almost due—not even out
of junior high.

And you and I know that that's not cool
but we act like it's alright to let her listen to
R. Kelly when she is not ready to understand that
R. Kelly is a grown man and wherever he and his
songs are probably taking her
He and his songs are probably raping her
And I like his music and I don't think he chooses to
come off like that
But reputations don't just come off like that
And TV stations don't just turn off like that
And what she doesn't know is . . . we get turned off
by that
When it comes down to choosing wives,
All those lies she had to tell
To sell herself
To tell herself
That those guys were going home with her
Just pride, not too many men have everything they
want
And don't already have wives
Ask R. Kelly, DMX, Snoop, or L.L.
And they'll tell her
It's just for sales and now the only thing she's sold is
herself and now she sees that when that man tells
her she's priceless he means just that—no cost at
all—and somehow she's lost it all
and what she doesn't know is he would have waited
because he has no choice but to
And the only thing sex sells is MTV that's how they
bought B.E.T.
but they won't tell her that
They'll just sell her this dream that the man she
wants has an SUV
and won't let her know he has a STD and a family
and I won't let her fall for that

What's most important in life
doesn't call for that
And if she's gonna make it big—which I know she
will—those clothes are too small for that
Cover that place and
What she doesn't know is if she makes up her mind
She won't have to make up her face
And some young woman will see her and want to be
her and someone's little sister and someone's
daughter and in this order she'll look in the mirror
and say "Someone wants to be me."
So she'll turn on the reading lamp and turn off the
TV and she'll read about Nefertiti or Gwendolyn
Brooks or Oprah and maybe she'll hope to make a
difference because
What she doesn't know is . . .
She isn't any different from any one of them
and she can be any one of them whenever she is
ready
But what she doesn't know is what she's gonna be—
But I do
And I'll do just about anything to see to it that if she
wants to, she'll do it.
By any means and I mean anything that it takes she's
gonna make it and I'll prove it
She's been through too much and I'll lose it if she
loses because of you or anybody else who doesn't do
what they can to help her move on, so move on if
you're planning to make no plans and I swear by no
chance will no man nor woman for that matter stand
in her way because she stands for something and
what she doesn't know is . . .
That matters

Let Me Speak for Him

For every disadvantaged youth
that never had an advantage
and will never utilize youth for its purpose
Will never realize his potential
Because it wasn't on the surface
He was never told to look inside of himself for worth
Rather shown that material wealth had more value
than morals and that synopsis is worthless but he's
still working on it

So let me speak for him
For every factory worker who knows what it's like to
just get by 23 years in a steel mill, blood, sweat and
tears to just get by
For what it's worth, he's always preferred hard work
instead of hanging on the corner to just get high
But he's still working on it
Day in and day out—living check to check—he's
gained so much respect from his kids
So let me speak for him

For every school teacher whose lesson plans include
real life
Who just doesn't teach curriculum, rather listens to
those kids and speaks to them
Knows not everyone woke up to clean sheets and
'Eggos'
Some sleep three deep on twin beds, one head in
between two sets of legs, space tighter than a
figure four leg hold and breakfast ain't Sunny Delight
and scrambled eggs
It might be the night's before egg rolls
So let me speak for him

For every preacher who does just that
Whether he's behind the pulpit or far from those
pews—anything aside from the word of God is far
from his views
because he views his position and desires to be held
accountable and know that the validity of his
message will impact a community a lot more than a
head count will do
So let me speak for him

For every sister who's never sacrificed her soul for
something because if there was one thing she was
taught it was that she could never be bought
so she's never fallin' for pickup lines because she's
picked up steam and just doesn't have time for that
until she gets older
Somebody once told me that she doesn't carry a
purse because she already has enough on her
shoulders
So let me speak for her

Let me speak for scores of children who just don't
know better and if someone doesn't speak up
They just won't know better
They don't know how to speak up because their
speech is impaired and through the fault of TV and
Ebonics, their speech isn't there
So let me speak for scores of children who do not
score well on standardized tests because they are
based on a standard that has never been tested
So let me speak for them

for every man who wants a woman who wants
something in life
She will not settle for anything less than a man with
a plan to make her his wife
Every man who's never cheated his vows never lets
the opinion of a few others clutter what's under his
brows he sees what's under her dress as a confession
to the commitment that they share and he
understands that it's not hard to get under the
covers of a woman who is under the impression that
sexy is showing off in clothes that show society her
underwear
So let me speak for him

For every drug addict, every alcoholic, every abusive
individual—whether to himself or unto others—no
matter what you call it
Every collect call from any of these to any of us
and even though we're tired of hearing how they've
changed their ways
We'll still put together bail money to bring them
home because we know that their problem is too
much, but jail is not enough to fix it
Their actions say stop me
Our ignorance would not listen...
In the lessons of their lives
Love was never mentioned
So let me speak for them

Let me speak for every old timer that can speak on
the good ole times
When Coca-Cola was 5 cents and a Big Mac was 5
cents and gas was 9 cents a gallon and school was a
5-mile walk up hill and every battle was uphill but
they made it

Every ounce of pride they could muster
They gave it
in hopes that we'd study our history to never
become slaves
For every grandparent that can't stand it when the
government takes away another dollar
I feel like Marvin Gaye, "Makes me wanna' holla!"
So let me speak for them

Let me speak for crack babies and those with AIDS
Young black brilliant brothers, especially those with
braids
Let me speak for every homeless homeboy and every
stranded sister
Every young man that understands the undertaking
that comes with wanting to be called Mister
Let me speak for the deprived,
the dissolute, and those in dire need
For every person who could not take the hits in life
so they tried weed
Let me speak for them
Let me speak for anyone who needs a voice of
reason—every man that cannot make up his mind on
what choice to believe in
Let me speak for him

Let me speak for anyone that is having fun right now
Anyone that just enjoys right now. Anyone that
maximizes the moment hopin' that peace of mind is
somewhere near
As long as someone hears me—let me speak for him
Let me speak for presidents, peasants and prisoners
Let me speak on every platform to every listener or
let me speak to someone who needs my words this
very instance

Let me speak for everyone who has words to share
but for some reason will not be heard
Let me speak in a universal tongue that touches
Third World countries, to inner-city suburbs and for
every soul that occupies space at one time or
another
For every young man that deserves to be given a
chance because he stands for something and doesn't
blame the dealer for the bad cards in his hand—as
fate would have it, he blames the success he's
attained on the loss of his mother

He knows, as long as he holds himself accountable
and is always responsible, he will change the way
the world works
The choice is not optional and if you believe then
there are no obstacles and to make this possible
Let me speak for him

Holy Spirit Breathe On Me

Holy Spirit breathe on me
When I'm out of breath with no more words
worthwhile not worthy
When there is no one left to hear my words
they've heard me no more stories to rejuvenate the
momentum
I was only given a few moments in which to spend on
my depiction of our existence as it relates to the
Scriptures,
I spent them couldn't waste time on each individual
hoping that a phrase I mentioned would speak on a
particular instance to a specific listener

For instance, in that one poem I broke down how
real men want women that want real men,
even gave a description, even went as far as to say
that I'd use every inch of air in my diaphragm to
diagram the blueprint to whom I am and any man
who can stand up and say he'll do the same can lean
on me, but right now I'm just out of breath

Holy Spirit breathe on me . . .

Lord, they say I should have made it already,
but they also say I am not humble enough
They say I am too young—I have not done it enough,
I am not worthy of my value,
but they say I will do great things
They say I am just what they need
Who are they?
I wonder if they bleed
Because they do not act like they know that I am
human

Besides a couple of paragraphs, minus a few pens,
I am you man
As I am not perfect
I just wish the world was
So I write about it in hopes that you will hear me
and tell me what you like about it
and maybe someone will hear my voice and voice
their opinion
And that is why I write
This is my religion and that is why I speak
The spoken word and hope it is heard because I have
faith
I do not believe these are the last days
So I do not want us to waste time telling people that
because they'll just give in
What is the hope of trying it if you are just going to
give in?
What is the message we are giving?
How can you say you have faith and say things like
these are the last days?
In so many ways that is not living
When the time comes, it will come and indeed we
will see and so I have spent most of my seconds
telling people that
So Holy Spirit breathe on me

Because I don't get much love in my home town
They cannot appreciate that what I talked about
then I am on now
but then—they appreciate my money
So, I think about what Jesus told Mary,
" . . . A prophet hath no honor in his own country."
So I keep writing
Rhyme and rhythm every ounce of will spent on
giving this testimony.

I know that he's not testing only me
Every setback and sideshow is only meant to show
me where my pride goes . . .
In Jesus, He might not show face in all I do,
But He sees it. So I will not let those backsliders or
non-believers
be the reason I did not make it into the Kingdom
For if any man thinketh he be without sin
bring him to thee and you'll will prove him a liar
When the nail touched my Savior's palm, he said
that I had the choice to never touch the
fire—and my mother's in Heaven—I have to see her
again.
So, I will pick up my cross as sure as these knees
will bend and spend my life trying to please
Oh, please, Holy Spirit breathe on me

Because it's all for you
Just give me a chance to advance and the proceeds
will go all to you
I can build an empire based on something else
But it will surely fall to you
So I am getting with the program
Getting what is mine
And giving it all to you
Every last step
Every last breath
You don't have to make it easy on me
As long as the Holy Spirit breathes on me

Stand

Stand for something
Or something will stand in the way
Of what you could have stood for

And if you don't stand for something in this life
Then what are you good for?

I have no problem
With so many people bending down
To their knees to pray

But if you would just stand straight up
It's a little bit easier for God
To hear what you are trying to say

Stand

You've fallen for the sickness
Of jealousy, ignorance, hatred, envy and greed
Well, if you've already fallen for what you don't
know
Why don't you Stand for what you believe?

Stand for Honor

Your Honor—
I don't need to take the stand to testify
I've already taken a stand and testified
That taking a stand was the best thing I've ever done
in my life

I've taken a stand against wrong
So I can stand to do something right

And if you are standing in my way
Then it's time for you to stand aside

My mother once told me that
Can't was not a word
Ain't was not a verb
And if I didn't stand for something I said
Then I'd fall for something I heard

So stand
She said I didn't need anyone's help
Because I could stand by myself
And if I couldn't stand on my own
I would have to stand on something else
Either you stand by your word or
You stand by yourself

A lot of us are just on standby
Just standing by
Letting this life just pass us by
And I don't understand why
Are you an innocent bystander
Or are you just standing by?

We lose the approval of God
By seeking the applause of man
So make up your mind to plan
Hold on with your hands
Get on your own two legs . . .
and . . .
stand
For something
Or fall for anything
But if you find something to stand for
Then you won't fall for many things

You may understand a lot, but you cannot stand for
anything

Stand
And you cannot stand against
The same thing you stand for
And you can't stand for anything less
If you can't stand anymore
Equality
Humanity
Freedom
And prosperity
Are just some of the things I stand for
And I can't stand those individuals who are not
against nor for
Take a stand
Be either or
Either against, either for
Once you find something to be eager for

STAND!

can you SEE?

DREAM, then DO!

Discussion Questions

For book clubs, speaking engagements, open mics, literary and special events.

1. How has this book inspired you?

2. Which poems reached out to you? Why?

3. The author believes that all living creatures can change. Do you believe that people want to change?

4. Do you feel that this author has a good knowledge of urban life and the world in general?

5. What emotions did you experience while reading this book?

6. What do you feel is the common or universal message in his poetry?

7. Do any of the poems closely relate to anything you may have experienced prior to reading this book?

8. What views or perspectives expressed by the author do you agree and disagree with?

9. How do you feel this book will help you and others?

10. Will this book help political leaders, mentors, healers educators and parents in a positive way?

11. How has this book changed your thoughts on society, parenting, culture, racial issues, etc.?

12. What will you start doing differently since reading this book?

W e hope you enjoyed this EbonyEnergy Book, *Writing With My Eyes*, as much as we enjoyed working with the author, **Cornelious "See" Flowers and his** management team for allowing us the opportunity to enter and share a very sacred place along the path as he continues his journey toward his big dream.

Writing With My Eyes can be ordered anywhere books are sold—bookstores, distributors and independent sales representatives. If you wish to receive a free catalog featuring additional EbonyEnergy Books and products or if you'd like information about the EbonyEnergy Literary Foundation, please contact:

EbonyEnergy Publishing, Inc.
P.O. Box 43476
Chicago, IL 60643-0476
(773) 779-8129 Office (773) 779-8139 Fax
Orders (Toll-Free 1-877-447-1266)
www.ebonyenergy.com

EbonyEnergy Publishing, Inc.

Check the website for Radio-Podcast, television appearances, lectures, workshops and locations.
Tune in to EbonyEnergy.com for the best in inspirational talk radio featuring top EbonyEnergy authors! And sign up via the EbonyEnergy.com Website to receive the EbonyEnergy online newsletter and stay informed about what's going on with your favorite authors like **See The Poet!** *You'll receive bimonthly announcements about: Discounts and Offers, Special Events, Products Highlights, Free Excepts, Giveaways, and more!*
www.ebonyenergy.com

About The Author

Cornelious M. Flowers, III

"See The Poet"

Born and raised in Chicago, Illinois. See is an author, speaker, mentor, healer and poet. His works have been featured in publications and on stages across the country. See's detailed bio is on the following page.

Go to his website www.seethepoet.com for Radio-Postcast, television appearances, lectures, workshops and locations.

Email: findme@seethepoet.com

Cornelious "See" Flowers

Spoken Word Artist

Can You "See"? An Evening With See The Poet

See has a message, and you will never experience anything like it. Featured on TLC's *The Messengers*, this self proclaimed "Performance Poet," possesses the rare quality that was recently described by a panel of judges for a television audition as, "One being one's gift." Combining hip-hop and a lot of divine inspiration, he brings to the stage his truth through a very cool version of a very ancient art.

Raised on the south side of Chicago, See is what many call "the real deal." Talent aside, his testimony reads like a script from a Hollywood movie. Every moment he has lived is both suspenseful and surreal, leading to the "never give up, never give in" attitude that See exudes. He has been flat broke and homeless. He didn't have a strong relationship with his biological father, and the mother he adored was murdered in 1994...and See found her body. He has also battled health issues, beating sometimes life-threatening hypertension for over a decade. And the list of seemingly insurmountable obstacles goes on. Nevertheless, See declares, "I'm writing for my life!" and follows his beloved mother's words telling him that he was born to "free his people." For See, that means pursuing his sacred mission of creating poetry.

With his eyes fixated on succeeding no matter what the odds against him, the journey will undoubtedly be a pleasure to witness and achieve. Through his company, What I See Entertainment, See continues writing and performing and has a book and spoken work CD in the works. He currently lives and works in Atlanta.

146

Printed in the United States
72198LV00002BA/220-363